You Deserve to Be Rich

Action Guide

Dennis M. Postema

The information contained herein is published for general purposes only. It is not meant to serve as an individual, personalized guide or suggestion.

Second Edition: April 2014

Introduction: 12 Steps to Success

"Success is not to be pursued;
it is to be attracted by the person you become."
—Jim Rohn

In my book *You Deserve to Be Rich: 12 Steps to Success,* I outlined a simple plan to help you find the right path toward achieving your goals. This action guide will help you work those basic steps. On the following pages, you'll find activities and strategies designed to help you:

1. Understand the rules of greatness
2. Define your dreams
3. Banish your fears
4. Think, live and breathe success
5. Create a vision
6. Set a purposeful path
7. Take action
8. Attract the right people
9. Make fair deals
10. Experience the power of giving
11. Be grateful
12. Keep moving forward

Wealth is not an unattainable goal. It doesn't matter whether you were born into a family with means or without, you deserve everything that the world has to offer. All too often we fall for the lies that tell us we're not good enough or that we don't deserve wealth because of who we are or where we come from.

The truth is, anyone can be rich. It doesn't require a fancy college degree, an intense work ethic or unbelievable intelligence. What it does require is an understanding of the science behind wealth and success. Because, at its core, wealth accumulation is a science. Break the code to that scientific strategy and you can become rich—no matter who you are.

Module 1: Understanding the Rules to Greatness

"Success is 20 percent skill and 80 percent strategy."
—Jim Rohn

Everyone has the capacity to achieve greatness. This is a simple fact. Some people seem to intuitively know this, and nothing will keep them from achieving that success. How can you become one of those people? The first step is to learn the rules for becoming rich:

Rule #1: You can be rich despite your current situation/environment.

What are some things in your current environment or circumstances that you've been blaming for your lack of success?

_____

_____

_____

_____

What can you do to work around them and reach your destiny?

_____

_____

_____

_____

Rule #2: Stop worrying that you lack the talent to succeed.

What are some small successes that you've had that didn't require talent as much as determination and strategy?

_____

_____

_____

_____

Who are some rich, successful people you admire who seem to have little in the way of talent outside of business management and strategy?

_____

_____

_____

_____

What skills can you learn to be more like them?

_____

_____

_____

_____

Rule #3: Stop blaming a lack of capital.

What can you do today that requires no money but puts you closer to your goal?

_____

_____

_____

_____

Write down four more steps you can take toward your ultimate goal for less than $100.

_____

_____

_____

_____

Rule #4: Stop looking for the perfect business.

What are you passionate about?

_____

_____

_____

_____

_____

What kinds of businesses can use the strengths, talents and knowledge that go with that passion?

_____

_____

_____

_____

Rule #5: Stop inventing obstacles to overcome.

Show yourself just how non-defeating so-called obstacles can be. Write down four obstacles and four ways to power through them or get around them.

_____

_____

_____

_____

Make a list of five people you admire.

_____

_____

_____

_____

Do some research on each of them. Write down at least one surprising fact on each.

_____

_____

_____

_____

_____

Taking Action

All of the above rules are related to nonexistent obstacles that many people allow to intimidate them. Are you letting any other perceived obstacles hold you back? If so, what are they?

_____

_____

_____

_____

Now, write down three ways you can overcome each of those obstacles.

_____

_____

_____

_____

Module 2: Defining Your Dreams

Dreams come in all shapes and sizes. Some people have small dreams while others believe in the old adage, "Dream big or go home."

When you want to become rich, your dreams are the gateway to success. Dreams alone, however, are not enough. You must define your dreams in order to map a path toward success. To find out what you should be pursuing, ask yourself these important questions:

1. What grabs my attention most?

_____

_____

_____

_____

_____

_____

_____

_____

_____

Not sure where you should begin when developing a plan for your future endeavors? Start by looking closely at those topics and activities that tug at your heartstrings or that excite you the most. Wherever your passion lies, use it to develop your own unique niche in the world of business.

2. What am I good at?

_____

_____

_____

_____

_____

Everyone is good at something. Whether you have a special talent or skill or a knack for doing something others find challenging, there is something that comes easier to you than it does to others. Focusing on things you're good at is a great way to lunge toward success.

3. What ideas keep nagging at me?

_____

_____

_____

_____

_____

Have you ever had an idea that you simply can't stop thinking about? That one may be the idea that needs investigating. No matter how impractical or silly it may seem to the rest of the world, figure out how to make that idea work. There's a reason why you can't get it out of your head.

4. How might you combine the above three points into a single, cohesive business idea?

_____

_____

_____

_____

_____

Now, let's focus on what you hope to ultimately gain. But let's go beyond the simplified concept of riches and get to the meat of the matter—what are your biggest dreams? Be specific—whether it's that new sports car, giant home or fat bank account, write down your innermost wants below.

_____

_____

_____

_____

_____

_____

Repeat this process, only this time, instead of focusing on material things, focus on the intangible benefits you want your wealth to afford you, such as time to do volunteer work or a general sense of security.

_____

_____

_____

_____

_____

_____

Finally, let's look at your career dreams. Do you want to run your own company? Be a high-powered executive at an existing company? Be an ideas person or a public speaker?

_____

_____

_____

_____

_____

_____

Using all the information above, create your personal dreams statement. Think of it like a mission statement for your ideal future. Write a clear, concise, two- to three-sentence statement. Avoid generalities.

_____

_____

_____

_____

Dealing with Dream Stealers

If you have a dream, then there is someone out there who wants to steal it. That's why you must protect those dreams as you would anything of great value.

You have to watch out for the people in your life who aren't on board with your plans. I like to call these people "dream stealers." These are the naysayers who thwart your attempts at greatness. Some do this emotionally or psychologically by telling you that you aren't good enough or don't have what it takes to attain your dream. Others are more sinister, actually doing things to stand in your way or cause you to fail at your attempts.

Regardless of what type of dream stealers are in your life, you must do whatever is necessary to protect your dreams. Here are a few ways you can do that:

Think about the people in your life who have, whether on purpose or otherwise, tried to steal your dreams. Name these individuals.

_____

_____

_____

_____

Consider the ways these dream stealers work. Do they make subtle comments that eat away at your confidence? Or do they sabotage your success in some other way? Write down a description of what they do below.

_____

_____

_____

_____

_____

_____

_____

_____

_____

_____

_____

_____

Now, come up with ways to counteract their attack. Maybe that means designing comebacks to their words, or simply recognizing what they are doing.

_____

_____

_____

_____

_____

_____

Evaluate your relationship with these individuals and consider whether it would be best to keep your distance from them.

_____

_____

_____

_____

If you find that a close friend or relative is always on the attack but that it's not practical to keep your distance, it may be time to seek either personal or family therapy. A trained counselor can help you see past their words and actions and stay on track with your own progress. Counseling may also help the other person see the damage they are causing.

Module 3: Banish Your Fears

What types of fear are holding you back? In the book, I mentioned fear of poverty and criticism. But it could even be more than that—a fear of success or failure could be to blame. Whatever it is, write it down below.

_____

_____

_____

_____

_____

_____

What is causing this fear? Is it from experiencing something like it in the past? Watching someone else deal with it?

_____

_____

_____

_____

If fear is the driving force keeping you down, it's time to break its grip. Learning to overcome your fears does not happen overnight but rather in small, incremental steps. To help you get started, try some of these valuable tips:

List four things that you're afraid of when it comes to going after your success.

_____

_____

_____

_____

Take the first item from your list and write down the absolute worst thing that could happen if it did indeed come true. Is it really that bad? If the answer is yes, then figure out some ways you could overcome the obstacles it creates.

_____

_____

_____

_____

Move onto the next item on your list and repeat the previous steps; then do the same for the remaining two items. Sometimes all it takes is facing your fears and creating a game plan should that fear become a reality.

_____

_____

_____

_____

_____

_____

_____

_____

_____

_____

_____

Finally, it's time to actually face one of your fears. Think of one thing you're afraid of that is holding you back in business. Figure out a way to face that fear head-on. For example, if you're terrified of giving speeches, schedule one. Start with just a short talk in front of a small group and work your way up. The point of this exercise is to face your fear so that it no longer holds any power over you.

_____

_____

_____

_____

Module 4: Think, Live and Breathe Success

An empire isn't something that just happens. It must be built, a process that requires persistence, perseverance and a state of mind devoted to tailoring efforts toward meeting a specific goal. In short, this means thinking, living and breathing success.

Think Yourself Rich

Is it possible to actually think yourself rich? Absolutely! It takes more than skill, education or even a plan to succeed. It takes the right attitude. You need to have the right thoughts and then turn those thoughts into action. For instance, if you allow negative thoughts to infiltrate your brain, your efforts will be more negative. But if you allow positive thoughts to overtake you, your efforts will be more positive—and positive actions always accomplish more than negative ones.

Some people call this type of thinking the law of attraction; others call it faith. Regardless of what you call it, this state of mind is essential to your success. So how can you develop it? Begin with the exercises below.

What are some common negative thoughts you have regarding yourself, your future and your potential for success?

_____

_____

_____

_____

_____

_____

_____

For each of the negative thoughts you listed, create a sentence that positively refutes it. Then, the next time you think the negative thought, stop and force yourself to repeat the positive one several times. For example, if one of your negative thoughts was that you don't deserve success, you might write the opposing statement, "Everyone has the capacity for success, and everyone deserves it." Then, the next time you start to think your negative thought, you can replace it and repeat the positive thought instead.

_____

_____

_____

_____

_____

_____

_____

_____

_____

_____

_____

Create a power board that illustrates your dreams. Tack up pictures of the house you want to buy, sayings that showcase positive thoughts and lists of things you want to accomplish. Write a plan for your board below.

_____

_____

_____

_____

_____

_____

_____

Make a to-do list. Thinking about what you want to achieve is not enough. Draw up a list of goals and action steps to take to get you where you want to be. Start every day with a detailed to-do list that is designed to move you closer to your goals.

_____

_____

_____

_____

_____

_____

_____

Three Forces to Rein In

There are three main forces at work that can either push you toward a positive outcome or stop your success in its tracks. They are: desire, belief and expectation. Here are some practical tips for reining in all three:

1. *Desire.* If you don't really have a desire for wealth, you'll never acquire it without some intervention such as an inheritance. That means that desire is both necessary and justified—but you need to keep those desires in check. List the things you're willing to do to become rich. Now, go through that list and cross off anything that can be construed as negative. For instance, if your list says things like:

   - Go back to school
   - Get any job
   - Look for an apprenticeship or internship to learn more about the business

This list may seem positive, but look more closely. "Get any job" could become a negative if you don't take one that aligns with your moral compass. Taking a job that involves illegal activity, shady or deceptive business practices or actions that you deem inappropriate can come back to bite you in the future, thus hurting your chances for success down the line. In addition, it won't make you feel good about yourself and that negativity will interrupt your progress. Consider all current and future consequences when considering new opportunities. Anything that isn't completely honorable should be avoided.

_____

_____

_____

_____

_____

_____

_____

_____

_____

_____

_____

2. *Belief.* Believing in yourself offers two benefits. First it boosts your confidence, which is the cornerstone of success. Second it helps to pull good things toward you. Likewise, a disbelief in yourself can push good things away. Sit down right now and write out a list of things you think you can accomplish and things you want (and need) to do but don't think you're capable of.

_____

_____

_____

_____

_____

_____

Consider how you can change these disbeliefs into possibilities. For example, maybe you can't sell homes right now because you're not trained to do so, but you can change that by getting your real estate license. The point is to figure out how to turn those disbeliefs into things you CAN believe in.

_____

_____

_____

_____

_____

_____

_____

3. *Expectations.* Desire and belief are essential to getting what you want, and so is expectation. Write down the expectations you have for each of your action steps and plans.

_____

_____

_____

_____

_____

On an index card, write down one thing you expect to accomplish this week. Carry the card with you, looking at it several times each day. Did you accomplish the task by week's end? If not, figure out why and then repeat the exercise next week, after you've removed the obstacle standing in your way.

_____

_____

_____

_____

Begin training your mind to think more positively. Listen to motivational tapes, read books on the subject and practice conscious positive thinking. It isn't always a simple task to reverse negative thoughts and allow positive ones into your conscious and subconscious brain, but it will set you on the right path toward success. Give yourself some ideas for getting started below.

_____

_____

_____

_____

Module 5: Creating a Vision

Everyone has dreams, some bigger than others. Many are eventually fulfilled and others are gradually abandoned. What makes one dream feasible and others unattainable? The first step to making your dream of wealth a reality is to create a vision that allows you to focus all of your energy and effort on it. It's your vision that helps you set the course on the road to wealth.

The first step to creating a concrete vision is to figure out exactly what you want. Sit down right now and figure out what it is you want to accomplish—don't be generic! Be as specific as you can about what you plan to accomplish in the next year, five years and 10 years.

_____

_____

_____

_____

_____

_____

_____

Think of some of the most important things you want to accomplish. Now, think bigger! Don't settle for what seems practical—reach higher. Most of us tend to underestimate our abilities, so when we expand our vision, we give ourselves the chance to achieve our true potential.

If your dream does not make you feel uncomfortable or downright terrified, then you have not dreamed big enough. Real dreams are meant to pull you from your comfort zone and make you stretch yourself in unimaginable ways.

Big:

_____

_____

_____

_____

BIGGER:

_____

_____

_____

_____

Write down your main dream. Now, how can you make that dream bigger? Maybe you want to open a small veterinary clinic. Now, expand that dream to include a full-service animal hospital, complete with an emergency room and/or abandoned animal shelter service.

This is my dream:

_____

_____

_____

_____

This is my dream on steroids:

_____

_____

_____

_____

_____

_____

Once you've created a vision for your future and expanded those dreams to include things you never considered possible, it's time to direct your energy toward a successful outcome. Focus = success. Without a clear focus, you'll wander aimlessly, grabbing hold of every opportunity but never really moving forward toward completion of your dream. Of course, focusing all of your attention and energy toward a single outcome isn't always easy. There certainly are a lot of things that can get in your way. Here are some steps you can take to avoid getting stuck:

Take an inventory of your personal and professional life. What things are distracting you from completing the tasks at hand? Is there too much on your to-do list? Find ways to cut those responsibilities. Find five things right now that you can cut from your daily or weekly schedule. Look for common, easily removed time wasters first such as television watching, going out with friends too often, etc. Then, move onto more difficult time takers such as grocery shopping (have your food delivered), cleaning (hire a maid), paperwork (hire an assistant), etc.

1. _____

_____

2. _____

_____

3. _____

_____

4. _____

_____

5. _____

_____

Get rid of the guilt. Guilt can sometimes keep us from true success. Success requires focus and focus like this requires your time, which means you may not be able to be as social as you once were. As long as you're striking a good balance between fun and work, guilt is unnecessary. Write down four things you can tell your friends and loved ones when they try to make you feel guilty about what you're doing.

_____

_____

_____

_____

Give yourself a pep talk. Our thoughts can propel us forward or stop us in our tracks. Take just five minutes each day to give yourself a pep talk. By taking just these few minutes to tell yourself you can do it, you are training your brain to think more positively.

Today's pep talk:

_____

_____

_____

_____

Module 6: Set a Purposeful Path

The path you set today will be the road you take tomorrow. That means that the road to success starts with a single step and if you don't know where to go, you're going to get lost.

Success doesn't come overnight and it rarely comes without a plan. Now is the time to map out your journey. Here are some steps to get you started:

To begin your journey toward wealth, you need to set goals, both short- and long-term. This means writing them down to review from time to time.

Start by writing out your ultimate goal. This is your perfect dream. Be specific.

My ultimate goal is:

_____

_____

_____

_____

_____

Next, break that goal into smaller goals, in the form of annual goals over a specific period of time. This is what I want to accomplish over the next 10 years in order to reach my ultimate goal:

1. _____

2. _____

3. _____

4. _____

5. _____

6. _____

7. _____

8. _____

9. _____

10. _____

In order to accomplish each annual goal, you'll need to break them down into milestones that keep you moving forward toward your annual and ultimate goals. For example, if you want to open a real estate office, your first major goal would be to study for, and then get your real estate license. Smaller milestones may be to study architecture and design, learn copywriting for better descriptions, land an internship or part-time job at a certain real estate office, etc.

Milestones to start my journey:

_____

_____

_____

_____

_____

_____

_____

Setting a purposeful path requires a plan of action. Designing that plan will take some time and thought. You may not usually be the kind of person who makes such long-term plans, but you'll need to start practicing these behaviors if you want to succeed.

Devising a plan doesn't mean being inflexible. Unforeseen opportunities will arise that should be evaluated. Likewise, unanticipated obstacles will require a calculated detour. That's okay. The purpose of your master plan is to give you a guide to follow to keep you moving forward.

Module 7: Taking Action

Positive thinking can only get you so far in life. Designing a plan can get you a bit further along the path toward wealth, but until you take some real action, your journey hasn't really started.

To become rich—no matter how you personally define that word—you're going to have to step forward and do some work. Really hard work. Sometimes this will come in the form of menial tasks that seem beneath your skill and knowledge. Do them anyway. Even the most insignificant task may lead to greater opportunity tomorrow.

Too many people settle for mediocrity at work. This is an attitude that holds them back. Step beyond the pack by showing that you are willing and eager to do any job, and those around you will take notice.

Look over today's to-do list. Does each and every item there impact your vision in some way, even if small? If not, consider why it remains on your list. Don't waste your time on things that do not advance your vision.

_____

_____

_____

_____

_____

_____

_____

Think about something trivial you have done in the last week or month that actually helped you step closer to your goal. Maybe you invited a coworker out for a drink only to learn that he knows someone who could be a valuable contact. Or maybe you offered a hand to another coworker when you weren't required to and that person put a good word in about you to the boss. Write these down to appreciate how every action can have positive and negative consequences.

A plan is only as good as the action is generates. If you spend all your time planning how you will get rich without ever getting to work building your bank account, you will never experience the true success that you're after, that you deserve. Look at your list of goals and milestones right now and choose one to get started on. Then, get to work to complete it. It doesn't have to be a big milestone. Even small steps move you forward. The important thing right now is to get started without delay.

Which did you choose? Write it down to hold yourself accountable.

Module 8: Attract the Right People

It's impossible to reach the pinnacle of success alone. Victory requires an entourage of help. Some people may think they reach the top all by themselves, but the truth is that it took a lot of help from a lot of people along the way to open up the opportunities for success.

You too need to surround yourself with the right kinds of people to ensure that you do not veer off course. In *You Deserve to Be Rich,* you learned about the different personalities you need to include in your team:

- *The Cheerleader*: Someone you can count on to encourage you along the way
- *The Devil's Advocate*: That person who isn't afraid to warn you when you veer off track
- *The Taskmaster*: The person who keeps you on track by pushing you forward through action rather than encouragement.
- *The Mentor*: The person who offers sound advice and his or her own experience to help you navigate the maze ahead of you

Figuring out whom to surround yourself with both professionally and personally while you work toward your goals is not always an easy task. Here are some exercises to help you build a strong team that you can depend on:

1. Make a list of the types of people you foresee needing in the next few years, those who complement your skills and pick up your slack. This can include an office manager, administrative assistant, PR manager and so on.

_____

_____

_____

_____

_____

Create job descriptions for these people. That way when the time is right to begin looking for help, you will know exactly what to look for. Include in your job description a checklist of the skills and personality traits you require from these individuals.

_____

_____

_____

_____

_____

_____

_____

_____

_____

_____

_____

_____

As you continue on your way toward riches, you'll be called upon to show strong leadership time and time again. Maybe you're a born leader, able to step into that role without concern. If you aren't, don't panic. You can begin now to build those leadership skills. Here are some simple things you can do to accomplish this goal:

What are some local leadership classes, seminars and workshops you can attend?

_____

_____

_____

_____

List your good leadership qualities and your not-so-good leadership qualities. Take one of those not-so-good qualities and begin work on improving yourself.

_____

_____

_____

_____

_____

_____

_____

_____

Write down some leaders you know and admire.

_____

_____

_____

_____

What lessons did you learn from them that you could incorporate into your own leadership style?

_____

_____

_____

_____

Write down a description of the kind of leader you want to be. Post this sentence or quote in a place you will see it every day. Strive toward that in all you do.

_____

_____

_____

_____

"Don't expect more from others than you are willing to give or do on your own."
—Anonymous

Module 9: Be Fair

Fairness is essential to your success. Not only should you expect fairness from those who deal with you, you should be fair and honest in your business dealings with others. This doesn't just mean your clients, but also your employees, subcontractors and those you purchase supplies, products and services from.

The world may tell you that success requires some degree of dishonesty, but you don't have to fall for that lie. Real success comes to those who show humility and compassion in their work and personal lives. Remember, positive thoughts and actions cause positive reactions, but the opposite is also true. What appears to be a good deal at the moment can turn very wrong down the line.

In *You Deserve to Be Rich,* you learned that humility and compassion are important components to dealing fairly with others. But how can you grow these traits? Here are some exercises to help you:

Who were some of the people involved in your last big success? Have you thanked them yet for their contribution? If not, list them below and take time to thank them today.

_____

_____

_____

_____

Make a list of five people who have been integral to your success in the last year. Write down what role each played in helping you overcome obstacles and reach your goal.

1. _____

_____

_____

_____

2. _____

_____

_____

_____

3. _____

_____

_____

_____

4. _____

_____

_____

_____

5. _____

_____

_____

_____

Write a quick thank-you note to each of the above individuals, acknowledging the part they've played in your life and business. Make sure the list includes both big and small players. Sometimes, we overlook individuals who seem uninvolved, such as the coffee vendor outside your office who always greets you with a smile and kind word (especially on those days you need them most).

Make a list of three times during the past year when you haven't accepted criticism gracefully. Outline ways in which you disappointed yourself in reacting to it. Study this list so you will be better equipped to handle such issues in the future.

1. _____

_____

_____

_____

2. _____

_____

_____

_____

3. _____

_____

_____

_____

Think of one person in your business or personal life who needs some compassion today. Consider something you can do to show them the compassion they deserve. It can be a big gesture or a small one—the size doesn't matter. What matters is that you express to them your willingness to see their hurt and you share your loving, kind spirit.

_____

_____

_____

Module 10: Give, Give and Give Some More

Do you make it a point to give of your time, talent, energy and money? If not, then you're missing out on a wonderful opportunity to increase your positive energy and do some real good in the world.

It doesn't really matter what amount of money or time you give. What matters most is that you make an impact on others though your generosity. Being a miser who hoards his or her money isn't going to accomplish anything. On the contrary, wealth should give you the freedom to share even more.

It's easy to find ways to give to your community. Here are some simple things you can do right now:

List several organizations you'd like to offer your expertise to. If they don't need your professional services or products, then roll up your sleeves and get to work helping in whatever manner they ask.

_____

_____

_____

_____

List any extra supplies or products that you can donate to a worthy cause. Think outside the box. Maybe you have some empty office space that you could allow a group to use, or maybe you would be willing to share your copy machine with a community group that doesn't have their own. No matter what you have available, I guarantee there is a nonprofit group out there somewhere that can use it.

_____

_____

_____

_____

_____

_____

_____

_____

Write down one day per month that you can make available to offer your services for free in the community. As a business expert, you can offer advice and guidance to other small businesses or those who are thinking of going into business. Or maybe you're a dentist who can give free cleanings to low-income and elderly folks. Think about unique ways you can offer your services and skills to others.

_____

_____

_____

_____

_____

_____

Write down a percentage of your profits that you are comfortable giving to the charitable cause of your choice:

_____

Module 11: Being Grateful

Gratitude is power. Without gratitude you can release no power and fewer good things will come your way. To clear this clog, you must acknowledge and show gratitude for what you already have.

Keep a gratitude journal. Every evening before bed, write down all the things that you have to be grateful for that day. The list can contain personal or professional things. Once you begin to list your praises, you will begin to see more and more of the blessings in your life. Begin now—list five things you have to be grateful for:

1. _____

2. _____

3. _____

4. _____

5. _____

Think of one thing that went wrong this week and write down all of the positive things that came out of the situation. Maybe your car broke down and you were late for work. But this event made you grateful you even have a car, or a job. Or that you can afford the mechanic who will fix it. Every bad situation can be turned into a good one with a little creativity and a change of mind and spirit.

_____

_____

_____

_____

Think of a negative incident that, in retrospect, turned out to be a good thing. Write down any other moments that show you how good can come out of difficult situations.

_____

_____

_____

_____

_____

_____

Choose to be grateful for one difficult situation in your life right now. Write a letter of gratitude or even a thank-you note to the universe for the experience and whatever you're learning from it.

_____

_____

_____

_____

_____

_____

Module 12: Keep Moving Forward

Building momentum means more than just moving toward your ultimate goal; it means finding innovative ways to use your resources in order to build your wealth. Take what you're good at and find new, unexpected ways to use that knowledge and talent to offer the world something even better. Use your ingenuity and resources to continue on the journey. Not only will this help increase your progress toward your goals, it will help you overcome obstacles and get unstuck.

Write down several ways to offer up your skills and talents to the world, such as by breaking into new industries or markets. Here are some examples of this philosophy at work:
- The owner of a gym decided to take his fitness knowledge and open a facility geared toward children. Understanding the dangers of childhood obesity, he designed programs that got kids moving in a fun way and helped them enjoy a more energetic playtime.
- A retired teacher saw the rise in homeschoolers in her area and began doing educational evaluations for the local homeschool community. Then she branched out, designing lesson plans for parents who decided to educate their children at home. As that business took off, she began adding services and now runs a successful academy-style facility, which offers a variety of homeschool classes including biology, chemistry, history and more.
- A local pet shop wanted to help keep the number of unwanted animals in the area to a minimum and began taking in strays. Soon they opened a separate shelter for abandoned and neglected pets. Before long they realized that more people would be able to keep their pets if they could find affordable healthcare options for these animals, so they enlisted the help of a local veterinarian who now offers low-cost vaccinations and spay/neuter services in a clinic set up in the basement of the shop.

It's your turn. Write down five unique ways you can expand your business by offering new services to a different clientele:

1. _____

_____

_____

_____

2. _____

_____

_____

_____

3. _____

_____

_____

_____

4. _____

_____

_____

_____

5. _____

_____

_____

_____

Module 13: Enjoying Your Success

You strive for wealth. Why? For most of us, a certain amount of money means we can enjoy life without the worries that accompany poverty. Yet, so many people fail to truly enjoy their money, even after they worked so hard to get it. Remember, your goal is to be rich but what does that mean to you? Describe in detail the life you hope to have once you've reached your goal. Describe the house you want, the trips you plan to take, the fun you expect to experience.

This is what I want when I'm rich:

_____

_____

_____

_____

_____

_____

_____

Write down five things you can do today to enjoy what you already have. Maybe you can't afford a cruise but you *can* afford to take 30 minutes to walk with a friend near the lake. Maybe an expensive shopping trip is out of the question, but an ice cream treat isn't. Don't put off having fun and enjoying the money you have at the moment. As your wealth increases, you'll have more opportunities to enjoy life's pleasures. But that doesn't mean you can't enjoy what you have right now with the people you care most about. Besides, the joy these activities bring will help to attract more opportunities toward you that can facilitate that future wealth you desire.

Things I'm going to do today or this week to have fun and enjoy today's riches:

1. _____

2. _____

3. _____

4. _____

5. _____

DESIGNING YOUR LIFE

What would happen if you discovered you could do more than just live your life—you could *design* it? This book teaches you to harness the power of your subconscious and program it to help you live a happy life fitting your definition of perfection.

DESIGNING YOUR LIFE: ACTION GUIDE

These exercises help you master your subconscious, abolish negativity and raise self-esteem. This guide focuses on creative visualization and powerful affirmations, to control your life's design and master your future.

DEVELOPING PERSEVERANCE

A combination of internal roadblocks are holding you back, preventing you from persevering. This book shows you how to break through these self-imposed obstacles to begin moving along your true path, taking you further than you ever thought possible.

DEVELOPING PERSEVERANCE: ACTION GUIDE

With this guide, you'll learn about the unique roadblocks you've designed for yourself and explore the thoughts, feelings and events that impact your ability to succeed.

YOU DESERVE TO BE RICH

If you're busy blaming your lack of wealth on upbringing, education and environment, you're missing out on learning how easy it is to get rich. This book teaches you to throw away the excuses and focus on the 12 steps to securing a future of financial success.

YOU DESERVE TO BE RICH: ACTION GUIDE

You deserve an ideal life. This workbook helps you get there by providing activities and strategies that explain the rules of greatness, help define your dreams and work to banish your fears.

UNLEASH YOUR MOJO

You already possess everything you need to be the person you want to be, you just have to access these powerful traits. In *Unleash Your Mojo*, you'll learn to recognize all the greatness inside you and discover how to put it to use and start living your ideal life.

UNLEASH YOUR MOJO: ACTION GUIDE

Each of us has power to succeed yet many of us never tap into that power. Instead we stagnate on the sidelines while others flash forward in life. This workbook gives practical tips, advice and exercises to advance in your quest for authenticity and power.

THE POSITIVE EDGE

There's a secret behind living a happy, successful, fulfilling life: *Positivity*. Learn how to overcome your tendency toward negativity, how to control your life and future, and how easy it is to improve your confidence and self-esteem.

SPARK: THE KEY TO IGNITING RADICAL CHANGE IN YOUR BUSINESS

A complete, step-by-step training program to help you become a high performer and higher earner. Learn how to rise to the top of your profession, position yourself as an expert and attract the abundance you desire.

DARE TO SUCCEED

Get the motivation and the information you need to rise to the next level of success! America's #1 Success Coach, Jack Canfield, has gathered together the top business minds in one powerful book. This guide contains their secret strategies to conquer the competition and bring ongoing abundance into your life.

VICTORY JOURNAL

The victory journal demonstrates the importance of writing down all your daily wins. Inside you'll find exercises to help define your ideal self and create action steps to move closer to your goals.

HARNESSING THE POWER OF GRATITUDE

 Recognize the positive energy moving through your day and harness it with this undated journal. Filled with inspirational quotes to help you maintain the spirit of gratitude, it's an ideal tool for developing an enduring, powerful habit of thankfulness.

APPRECIATING ALL THAT YOU HAVE

 This 365-day journal filled with inspirational quotes provides a safe space to write down the many things you're thankful for. It's the perfect way to help shift your perspective and recognize the abundance of positive forces in your life.

THE PSYCHOLOGY OF SALES: FROM AVERAGE TO RAINMAKER

 Take your sales from lackluster to rainmaker without any smarm, aggressive tactics or dishonesty. This book teaches sales pros the psychology of their customers so they can present products the right way for each shopper.

THE PSYCHOLOGY OF SALES: ACTION GUIDE

 In this action guide, you'll gain greater insight into your own personality and psychological makeup as well as that of your customers so you can further your sales success and transform your career.

RETIREMENT YOU CAN'T OUTLIVE

Cut through the hype and challenge conventional wisdom with a book focusing on conservative and reasonable ways to save for retirement. This book uses plain language and lots of common sense that's been missing from financial planning sessions for decades.

RETIREMENT YOU CAN'T OUTLIVE: ACTION GUIDE

Transform the lessons taught in *Retirement You Can't Outlive* into action steps that change the shape of your financial future. This immersive tool contains worksheets, exercises and review sheets to help you develop a plan to rescue your financial future.

NAVIGATING THROUGH MEDICARE

Don't be confused by the rules, plans and parts of Medicare. This book simplifies the complex system and allows you to quickly and easily make the right decision for the future of your healthcare. It's a one-stop guide to everything you need to know.

AVOIDING A LEGACY NIGHTMARE

Poor planning can rip your estate from your loved ones. *Avoiding a Legacy Nightmare* is a simple guide to help you get started in creating an effective estate plan that achieves all that you intended.

PHYSICIANS: MONEY FOR LIFE

If you want to retire on your own terms, you must understand the special considerations that physicians need to make in order to maintain sustainable retirement plans. *Physicians: Money for Life* casts aside traditional advice that's not suited to conservative retirement planning and focuses on helping physicians design a plan that creates money for life.

PHYSICIANS: MONEY FOR LIFE: ACTION GUIDE

You have the knowledge necessary to change the financial health of your retirement, now it's time to apply it. This action guide helps you transform the lessons taught in *Physicians Money for Life* into action steps you can take to change the shape of your retirement. With worksheets, exercises and review, this guide will help you move forward in your retirement planning journey while devising a plan to save it.

ALZHEIMER'S LEGACY GUIDE

Alzheimer's patients and their caregivers face a race against the clock and must learn how to cement a well-thought-out legacy plan before the disease's mental, emotional and psychological effects start to take their toll. This book provides guidance to both the recently diagnosed and those who will care for them as the disease progresses.

FINANCING YOUR LIFE: THE STORY OF FOUR FAMILIES

This is the story of four families that took their financial lives out of the red and into the black. There's McKenna, a single mom of two boys, working hard every day as a waitress; Toby and Shannon, two professionals battling a layoff and personal spending demons; Blake and Christine, a newlywed couple in a hurry to start living the good life, whether they can afford it or not; and Marcie and Kurt, two young parents struggling to keep up in an increasingly image-obsessed society.

FINANCING YOUR LIFE: THE WORKBOOK

Financing Your Life is an innovative workbook devoted to teaching you how to take total control over your financial life. Within, you'll learn about the secret behind financial planning, budgeting basics, insurance, credit repair, getting out of debt, developing financial compromise with a spouse or partner, saving and investing, mortgages and more.

This tool does more than just tell you about financial concepts; it helps you begin immediately integrating what you learn into your own financial life.